Momma's Sayings

*Things My Momma Said
and Maybe Yours Did, Too.*

WISDOM. TRUTH. HUMOR.

Copyright © 2025 by Kandra Albury

All rights reserved. No part of this book may be reproduced or transmitted in any form or by any means without written permission from the author.

ISBN: 9798989850723

Introduction

Simply put, my momma *is sweet as sugar, and stronger than steel.* Not only do I dedicate this literary work of my mom's saying to my queen mom, but to all mothers [and mother-like figures] who are on the special assignment of motherhood.

It is on this journey that mothers discover infinite wisdom, indescribable strength, and unconditional love for their forever babies. The goal— to ensure their children experience successful, gratifying, safe, and sustainable lives as productive human beings…a life that will make their heart smile.

However, the life-long journey of motherhood comes with countless sacrifices of themselves, their hopes, and dreams just to ensure their children's needs are met [and sometimes exceeded]. In many cases, this means that moms must choose to become what they didn't have— an improved version of their beloved mother.

Moms do their best, even when their best isn't good enough. They try to protect their children by adopting traditions; thereby, becoming rookie researchers seeking knowledge and solutions to raise *whole* children.

Momma, this was you! You did your best and for that we thank you. We appreciate your countless sacrifices, wisdom, truth, and humor.

Thank you for instilling in us the importance of always doing our best, being persistent in prayer, and dutiful in service to our families, God, jobs, and our communities. We are who we are because of you.

You truly are "blessed by the best" and so are we!

"Don't put nothing before God."

"It'll take God to save you, and it's gonna take God to keep you."

"If you get serious with God, God will get serious with you!"

On Sundays: "We're going to the Lord's house, today, to give Him some of our time!"

"God gave y'all to me to raise, and with the help of the good Lord, I'mma do just that!"

"There are three houses: our house, God's house, and the schoolhouse...Act like you have some sense at all of 'em!"

"I have to get up to cut fern, and y'all got to go to school—everybody has a job to do!"

"It's not what you say but how you say it."

"I send you to school to learn how to read."

"Those teachers got their education, now you got to get yours!"

"Don't be out to that schoolhouse showing out. You go to school to learn!"

"Y'all are in Emily's army now! My job is to train you up!"

"If you want something to play with, you better go to Pic'N Save and get you a toy…'cause I ain't no toy!"

"I'm not mean. I just say what I mean and mean what I say!"

"God gave you a behind so I can beat it!"

"If you don't stop that crying, I'm going to give you something to cry about!"

"I'm going to whip you for the old and the new!"

"I whip you because
I love you."

"This behind cutting is going to hurt me more than it's going to hurt you!"

"When I'm dead and gone,

see about one another."

"Bath time is 6 o'clock!"

"Treat people the way you want to be treated."

"You don't say or do things to hurt people's feelings."

"Your word is your bond."

"You were born by yourself–
so be by yourself!"

"Don't let nobody make a fool out of you!"

"If your friends rob a bank, and you're with them, you're going to jail, too!"

"Because your friends go and jump off a mountain, don't you go and do it!"

"Trouble is easy to get into,
and hard to get out!"

"Let people talk. They will talk about you when you're doing good and when you're doing bad…People are going to talk about you when you're dead and gone!"

"A bullet doesn't know nobody!"

"Those people are looking for the same thing I'm looking for –money!" *

* Whenever the fair would come to town

"If you don't have any money, then stay your Black behind home!"

When we would ask for fast food but money was tight

I have your Burger King and your McDonald's right at the house! "

Mom would pat out hamburgers and make French fries in our kitchen.

"Don't look down on others because you never know who you'll need."

"Some people don't have a pot to pee in or a window to throw it out!"

"You reap what you sow!"

"Just keep on saying good morning."

"Keep your hands to yourself, but if someone hits you, first, hit 'em back!"

"Don't hold grudges."

"You're going to see some things before you leave this world."

"Some people will suffer before they leave this earth!"

"You have your people mixed up with that tone!"

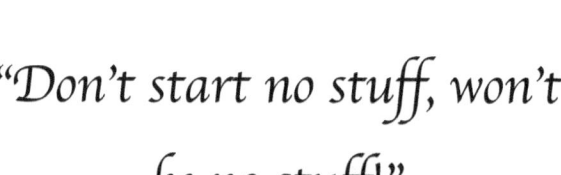

"Don't start no stuff, won't be no stuff!"

"If I have to scuffle to raise you, you're going to do what I say!"

"Do what I tell you to do the first time!"

"Keep talking back, and you'll have to go to the part shop across the street for some teeth." [part shop AKA: the cemetery].

"Keep making noise, while I'm driving, and I'm going to make you walk home!"

"If you mess up, cleanup–we don't have a maid service!"

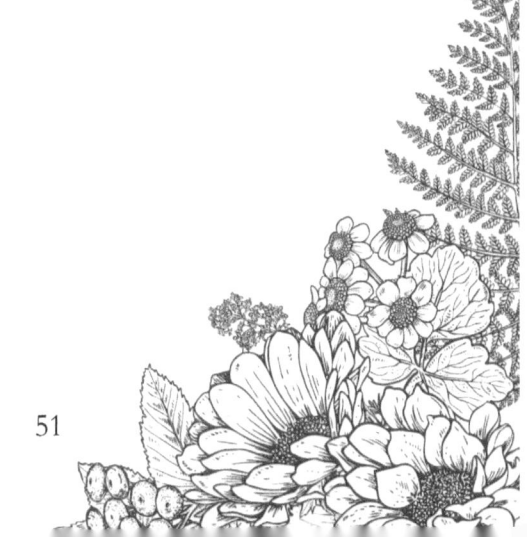

"Don't be smiling and grinning in married men's faces because you wouldn't want another woman doing that to your husband."

"God sits high and He looks low, beholding the good and the evil."

"You can fool some of the people some of the time, but you can't fool God none of the time!"

"Do not mess with quiet people because they'll hurt you."

"When people don't want to be bothered, let them be!"

"Don't leave one job until
you have another one."

"Don't give anything to someone that you wouldn't want yourself."

*"If it doesn't concern you,
keep your mouth closed!"*

"Keep your nose out of other people's business."

"You have to see and don't see."

"When somebody asks you something, say, 'I don't know!' You can't make nothing out of I don't know!'"

"People don't want to be around you if you act ugly…They'll hate to see you coming and be glad to see you go!"

"Don't get caught up in mess, and keep your name out of mess!"

"Don't go against your raising."

"Keep it moving, honey!"

"It's better to give than to receive."

"Don't be stout-hearted."

"Fix yourself up when you go out; you never know who you're going to meet."

"You go to work to pay your bills…nothing should be getting cut off."

"When you work hard for something, you'll appreciate it more!"

"Do your work right the first time and you won't have to do it again."

"I don't want to see any inadequate preparation on your report cards, because I buy plenty of paper and pencils for you to get your lesson!"

"Speak to people when you see them; even a dog says good morning by wagging its tail."

"When you get an education in your head, no one can take it from you."

"Watch how you treat me because you will need me before I need you."

"Don't let your mouth write a check your behind can't cash!"

"Don't look in grown people's mouths when they are talking!"

"One monkey don't stop no show!"

"If you eat too much candy,
your teeth will rot right out
of your head!"

"Don't sit too close to the TV, or you'll go blind."

"Don't keep coming in and out—either stay in or stay out!"

"Wash your hands before you go into my kitchen!"

"Close my refrigerator door!"

"What won't kill you will surely make you stronger."

"Don't believe their lies...Boys tell every girl she's cute."

"Answer grown people yes ma'am and yes sir."

"Respect will take you further than money."

"Respect is due to a dog."

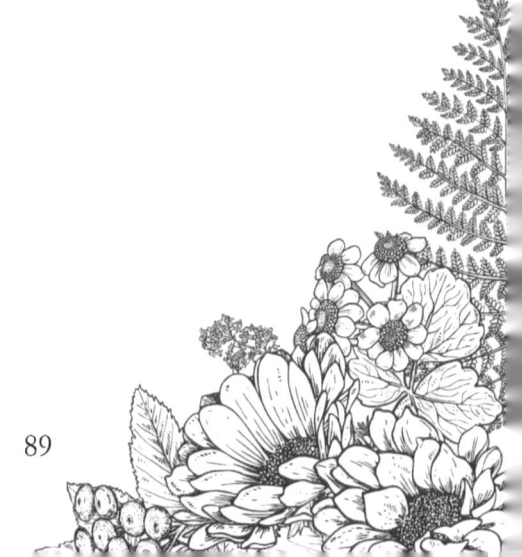

"Don't let nobody tell you what you can't do!"

"Don't let your left hand know what your right hand is doing!"

"Answer when I call you!"

"If you can't hear,
you can feel."

"Even if you don't have but a dollar in your pocket, act like you have a million!"

"Something is always better

than nothing!"

"Tell God thank you for this food because somebody somewhere doesn't have food to eat."

"I want that plate clean as my hand!"

"This house better be spic'n span when I get back here!"

"Don't open anything new,
until all the old is eaten up!"

"Don't let nobody come and take over where you stay!"

"Say thank you because people don't have to do anything."

"Say excuse me when you step over someone, or you need to get by."

"Don't let dark
catch you outside."

"Go cut me a switch!" (I'd always bring back a twig)

"If you lie, you'll steal, and
if you steal, you'll kill!"

"When you go in the store, don't take nothing out of there if you didn't pay for it!"

"Birds of a feather flock together!"

"Don't follow the crowd because the crowd ain't always right!"

"A dog that brings a bone
will take one."

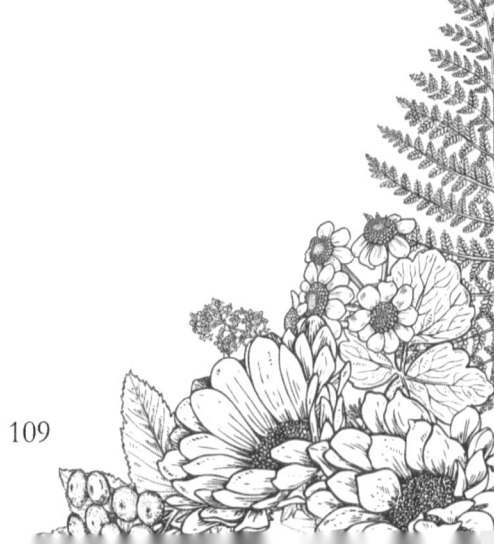

"Don't follow up behind foolishness!"

"Roll your eyes at me again and they'll be rolling on the floor!"

"You can draw bees better with honey than you can with vinegar!"

"Sit up straight- don't slouch!"

"Stop dragging your feet when you walk –you sound lazy!"

"Walk like you got somewhere to go!"

"The truth will overtake a lie every time!"

"Nothing from nothing leaves nothing."

"What you put in, is what you get out; nothing more, nothing less."

Thank God for the Little Things

by Emily June Williams

Thank you, God, for little things that often come our way

The things we take for granted but don't mention when we pray.

The unexpected courtesy. The thoughtful, kindly deed– a hand reached out to help us in the time of sudden need.

Oh, make us more aware, dear, God, of little daily graces that come to us with sweet surprise from never dreamed of places.

About the Author

Kandra Albury is a servant leader, peace diplomat, author, children's advocate, business, and life solutionist. She is also the Co-CEO and Founder of More Than Expected (MTE) Publishing, a full-service publishing agency in Gainesville, FL.

She is the founder and CEO of Kids'n Capes, Inc., an organization that serves as a catalyst to community members, donors, and organizations to help prevent and raise awareness of sexual abuse, bullying and illegal drug use in children early on.

She earned a Bachelor's degree in communication from the University of North Florida and a master's degree in mass communication from the University of Florida.

She has a Ph.D. in ministerial education from Truth Bible University, and is the assistant pastor at Ministry in the Word Outreach International. She has more than 15 years of corporate communication experience. Kandra serves as the VP of Marketing with Meridian Healthcare, Inc.

In September 2023, Kandra released her most anticipated literary work, "Extravagant Peace." In 2012, she published her memoir *"From Food Stamps to Favor."* Immediately after publishing her first book, she released the signature book in her children's book series titled, *"Don't You Dare Touch Me There!"* This book has been read to more than 5,000 children and adults in Florida, Georgia, Texas, Colorado and Kigali, Rwanda (Africa). Her literary and children's advocacy work has been featured in numerous print publications as well as on local, national, and international television networks such as WCJB-TV-20, WUFT, WJXT-Channel 4, African Network Television-ANTV (host of the Kids'n Capes Show) and Trinity Broadcasting Network (TBN), the largest Christian network in the world.

Kandra is married to James C. Albury, director of the Kika Silva Pla Planetarium at Santa Fe College. They are honored to be the parents of three amazing children and three awesome grandchildren.

She is a member of Zeta Phi Beta Sorority, Inc. Gainesville's Delta Sigma Zeta Chapter.

www.ingramcontent.com/pod-product-compliance
Lightning Source LLC
LaVergne TN
LVHW041612070526
838199LV00052B/3111